SOLIO

SEAGULL
BOOKS
·
CELEBRATING
40 YEARS

THE AFRICA LIST

Samira Negrouche

SOLIO

TRANSLATED BY

Nancy Naomi Carlson

LONDON NEW YORK CALCUTTA

Seagull Books, 2024

First published in French in two volumes
as *Quai 2|1, Partition à trois axes* and *Traces*

© Samira Negrouche, 2019, 2021

First published in English translation by Seagull Books, 2024
English translation and foreword © Nancy Naomi Carlson, 2024

ISBN   978 1 8030 9 338 3

British Library Cataloguing-in-Publication Data
A catalogue record for this book is available from the British Library

Typeset at Seagull Books, Calcutta, India
Printed and bound in the USA by Integrated Books International

CONTENTS

FOREWORD

I was first introduced to Samira Negrouche by Patrick Williamson, a poet, translator, professor, friend, and editor of *The Parley Tree: Poets from French-Speaking Africa and the Arab World*, an anthology that led me to translate Khal Torabully and Abdourahman Waberi. Patrick asked me to translate poems by Negrouche as well as work by Tanella Boni and Vénus Khoury-Ghata as part of a supplement focusing on francophone poetry from Africa and the Arab world. I was excited at the prospect of expanding my focus beyond sub-Saharan Africa, and at the opportunity to translate francophone women authors, whose voices are largely outnumbered by their male counterparts. These co-translations with Catherine Maigret Kellogg, including Negrouche's "11," were published in *The High Window* in 2022, where anglophone readers were introduced to the timeless speaker of the poem, reclaiming histories and memories:

> I came from that time that amasses horizons and
> sifts through them, one by one, with care
> giving each its measure.

Translating "11" whet my appetite to translate more work by Negrouche. Considered a major voice in Algerian poetry, Negrouche lives and works in Algeria, having made the decision, over twenty years ago, to pursue a literary career over continuing to practice medicine. She represents a new generation of Maghrebin francophone poets who have chosen to write in French, the language of the colonizer. She compares the violence and trauma inflicted on Algeria to rape, yet maintains that French is a part of her, just like rape victims carry foreign DNA in their bodies. Hers is an *Algerian* French, distinguished by the legacies of multiple dynasties and empires that ruled over this region.

In addition to her Algerian compatriots, Negrouche counts among her influences Etel Adnan, Nicole Brossard, and Rimbaud. She also includes René Char, which is perhaps another reason I was drawn to her work, as I've translated two Char books. Music and mystery are common denominators in their poetry.

Solio is actually two books in one, containing two full-length volumes that have never before been translated into English: *Quai 2|1, Partition à trois axes* [*Quay 2|1: A Three-Axis Musical Score*], first published in 2019, and *Traces* [*Traces*], first published in 2021. Both books represent collaborations with other artists: the former was created with violinist Marianne Piketty and theorbist Bruno Helstroffer, while the latter was created with choreographer Fatou Cissé. Indeed, the second section of *Quai 2|1* is meant to be read as one poem, long as a river, which echoes the second movement of Philip Glass's Concerto for Violin and Orchestra No. 1. Although these books owe their existence to collaborations, Negrouche, in her afterword to *Quai 2|1*, was adamant that her writing be able to stand on its own: "I felt it was important that the work feed off the music's soul, but also be a poem, free of any context."

Solio is loosely ordered around the theme of movement, with the texts structured as poetic sequences containing no titles, except for those from *Traces* designated by their chronological appearance. The language is multilayered and evocative, approaching the surreal. The "you's" and "I's" are intentionally left nameless, ambiguous, and fluid, which renders them more universal. Indeed, the "I's" contain multitudes, their voices intertwining on the page where gesture becomes "multifold" (p. 102):

You see them move forward, the pilgrims have neither height,
nor age, nor gender, nor color. And yet, you see they're every-

thing at once, you see they're a merging multitude now adopting the same facial expression, the same muscular contraction.

One of the major translation challenges I faced was how to handle the words that appeared multiple times in the book. My dilemma was whether I should render them the same everywhere they occurred, for the sake of consistency, or switch up the meanings, depending on the context. To help with my thought process, I drew on Margaret Sayers Peden's assertion that while she tried to be consistent in how she translated the same word, she also believed that "the same word, given the fact that words are slippery and treacherous, *needs* to be translated differently within different contexts." In the end, I decided to translate the recurring word as consistently as possible, while also considering its place in the line, the sequence, and the entire work. In order to honor the music of the original French, I paid particular attention to maintaining any patterns of assonance, alliteration, and rhythm I discovered through applying a strategy I call "sound mapping." The overwhelming sound patterns I identified in *Solio* involved the repetition of words and phrases which contributed to the rhythms driving the entire collection, imbuing the book with its own internal momentum.

Words referring to movement were among the words that were most frequently repeated. For example, some form of "traverser" (which can mean "to pass through," "to cross," "to go through," "to traverse") occurred over thirty times in this collection. In many cases, the choices seemed interchangeable, but my task was to choose which of these translations would work best for the majority of cases. I noticed that "*pass* through" seemed a more effective way to evoke ancestors who had already passed on to another dimension than "*go* through." Once I'd made that decision, I ruled out the use of "cross," as it carried the distracting connotation of "opposing" or "standing in the way of something." The diction of "traverse" seemed a bit too lofty to my ear. In addition, "traverser" in "2" (p. 83) is used to refer to a forest the "you" is passing through, but later in the same section, "traverser" is used to refer to the forest "passing through" the "you." I felt the same translation needed to be used for both of these instances, and semantically speaking, "passing through" seemed a better choice.

> Coarse walls whose gray verges on apoplectic, walls piled near the trunks, near the shadows, near the trees, near the inert clouds, against the open angles of the forest passing through you. . . . It depends on how you pass through.

Because of this one instance that clearly swayed me to use "pass through" over "traverse," I tried to be consistent in using "pass through" throughout the English translation, unless there were extenuating circumstances. For example, in several cases, "traverser" was used in the context of a body of water, so I chose the more fitting "cross," as in this example, in "4" (p. 89):

> I don't want to remember that the sea is a wall /// I'm not trying to cross the sea ///   I don't want to remember that the sea doesn't want me to cross it . . .

The example below demonstrates an instance where I chose "traverse" in order to replicate the t-alliteration in the original (p. 18):

> Quand la ronde s'ouvre
> frémis au-dedans
> **t**oi par qui le **t**emps
> s'arrê**t**e
> **t**oi qui a **t**raversé
> le **t**emps

When the round opens
quiver inside
you through whom **t**ime
s**t**ops
you who've **t**raversed
time

In addition to the many words that made multiple appearances in this volume, so, too, did certain phrases. One of the most memorable ones involved this intentionally unusual phrase: "ça me tousse," which literally means "it coughs me." The issue was not only how to translate it in the multiple places where it appeared, but a secondary conundrum arose that involved an issue often faced by translators: where on the continuum of strangeness and familiarity should the translator land? On the one hand, if the translation sounds too strange, it can disrupt the flow of the text, and the translation may seem amateurish. On the other hand, if the translation only sounds fluid because it's been smoothed out, the translator may have missed an opportunity to showcase the author's unique style. In this case, I decided to maintain the unconventional meaning of the French for its initial occurrence, because of its contribution to the rhythm and playfulness of the sequence. Because its structure was parallel to the adjoining lines, the phrase didn't seem to greatly impact the fluidity of the translation, as in the example that follows (p. 25):

j'avance
dans l'éternuement du jour
ça me tousse dans les oreilles
ça me gratte dans les yeux
ça éternue partout
ça tousse
ça hoquette

I move
into the sneezing of daylight
it coughs me in the ears
it scratches me in the eyes
it sneezes everywhere
it coughs
it hiccups

In keeping with Negrouche's impulse toward "the strange," I decided to title this collection *Solio*, a word which first appears in "11" (p. 110), the book's final section, and is repeated six times, reaching a crescendo when the "I" makes an astonishing revelation. This enigmatic word carries multiple meanings. In Ido (Esperanto) it means "threshold." It also echoes words from other languages and cultures, including "sol" in Spanish, meaning "sun" (a very strong symbol in Algerian and African poetry) and "solium" in Latin, meaning "seat" and "throne." It also is a word from the Malinke oral tradition in West Africa, used by griots to ask for the audience's attention and serves as an apt ending to this collection, as well as the perfect invitation to read it.

Solio!

Nancy Naomi Carlson

QUAY 2|1

A Three-Axis Musical Score

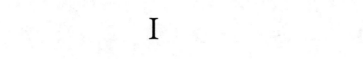

I

I haven't been gifted to see
what slumbers in oblivion
I come from that unsaid elsewhere
I move in an unwritten elsewhere
I move forward
my footsteps supported by doubt
an invisible thread between my fingers

and I brush past you

and I seem to brush past you

my arms cross seas

my roots have no anchor

my roots are out of season

don't search for a trace of my voice

through you it gathers

through you it unfurls

I even accept the illusion

for us it's a spark

a rousing twilight

a star we invent

a word we hide

but laziness doesn't suit you
laziness soothes nothing
worth lingering around

I pass so far from you
when you clench your fists
and consider my silence
I pass so far from you
so far from us.

I haven't been gifted to see
what pulsates in the wall
I move toward you through my pulse
through an unwritten memory.

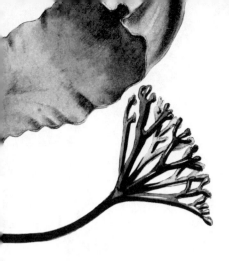

I'm rooted in movement
the cobblestones soaked in night
remember me
I'm rooted in a moment's wandering
the address of a marine window
that knows how to ignore the debris
my decomposition means little to me
when I'm rooted in movement
the roof of the old city
is my home.

I haven't been gifted to hear
the fire crackling in the distance
I live in the white dawn
I slumber in the cool breeze
my gaze doesn't wait
it marvels at the moment

the white surface isn't the void

nothing isn't the void

what's unsaid about us

isn't the void

I'm not afraid of what's unsaid

nor of the breach concealing time

it's the din of the world that frightens me

the din of nothing which isn't nothing

the din of the bloated void

that inhabits sidewalks

and then streets

and then parks

and then your room

and then your head

I'm not afraid of emptiness

the breach is a distant moment

a sun being reborn

in the cool surface

of a silent morning in winter

where I want to think of the nothing that opens

where I want to think of the space that remains

where I want to believe

that on a snowy trail

a breath lands

and sets down fear.

I approach the highest riverbank
by the narrowest path
a rope knotted
backwards

I approach the retreating wave
my posture unstable
legs flexed

I approach a dream
an attraction

I totter
I totter

has anyone ever known
how to walk
in daylight?

I always move
on an uncertain thread
on a certain rupture
and I offer my voice
as I'd offer my cheek
I lengthen my stride
like brushing against
a threshold

I'm not afraid
of the day that goes by
nor of the beings who
no longer go by

I'm not afraid of emptiness
emptiness isn't nothing
emptiness is along the thread
the uncertain thread
the invisible thread
on which I suspend existence
on which existence suspends me
wherever it happens
wherever it clings
wherever you approach
the quay

I barely move forward
footsteps suspended
on the oily surface

or it's the quay
that moves forward
breaks loose
drifts away
on the leathery skin
the indomitable skin
with reflections of silver

or it's my gaze
that glides
gets closer to
the quay
brings me closer
to the quay

I go naked
in the onion fields
and in the lush jungle
in the underworld
of Mexico City
Ouagadougou
and Aden
I go naked
my joints unrestricted
my back straight
I sway
my back broad
my neck light
my neck taut

the day finds a way
into my precocious
eyes

a lunatic dances
in my eyes
makes my hands
wobble
on the air sailing
in the sky
that consents to be painted

a lunatic dances
or I dance
when the round opens.

When the round opens
quiver inside
you through whom time
stops
you who've traversed
time

may your curve
smooth out
at daybreak

May the new wind
come
may the murmur
announce itself

quiver outside
may your face
pass through
all
light.

Let the wind
sculpt your eyelids
the day's clamor
inhabit your breath
let your chest
welcome the echo
let your body
regain its rhythm
let

may the gaze
pass through
may the hand
pass through
may the voice
pass through
may the gaze
pass through
may the hand
pass through
may the voice
pass through
open.

II

I move

into the sneezing of daylight

it coughs me in the ears

it scratches me in the eyes

it sneezes everywhere

it coughs

it hiccups

what spreads among us

is a repetitive

humming

on an irregular cycle

it rotates chaotic

it coughs on me

it scratches me

it sneezes

especially on my neck

I don't know who's blowing

on my neck

I don't turn around

it coughs

it hiccups

I don't know

who's speaking

I can't tell

who's passing by

I forget myself

in the sneezing of daylight

I move
with uneven steps
a humid din
in my ears
it coughs
it hiccups
you haven't spoken to me
about your mother
apparently Hungarian
and a Spanish teacher
on a secondary road
in Auvergne
I move forward
are you coughing inside me
while I move forward?
It's cold
I'm not sure
I hear
the story about your mother
when it's cold
I'm not sure
I can calculate fast enough
the cycle's irregularity
when it's so cold
that it goes through the thighs
that my torn jeans
shiver the thighs

what have you put
in my ears?
It's the obvious cycle
it sometimes hums
but more often than not
it squeals
it sneaks off
it's so cold
that I don't hear you anymore
you said the sea?
Do you want to swim
in the sea?
In a pink and pistachio
wetsuit?
I'm pretty sure
my guardian angel
is allergic
to pistachios
and probably
to pink
to the color of course
he likes
to be virile
my guardian angel
can handle everything
but not pink
not canary yellow

not orange either
Ah! But you still
are coughing
on my neck
you know very well
I can't
turn around
why are you coughing
on my neck?
The wind effect
paralyzes
my joints
my trunk
is frozen
by the wind effect
don't cough on me
especially when you're talking
about your mother
I wish I had
known your mother
talked to her about my
guardian angel
served them something sweet
and some almonds
but not pistachios
I'm pretty sure he's actually
allergic

to pistachios
and to pink
the color of course
everything that's pink
even flamingos
and lakes
especially lakes
he doesn't like humidity
yet can handle everything
my guardian angel
is virile
very virile
in appearance
he might almost like pink
he's not afraid of pink
he's not afraid . . .
my angel
might gladly have tea
with your mother
but for
the humid din
in my ears
if only
you weren't coughing
in my ears
I could hear
the story of your mother

from Hungary
your professor mother
who speaks Spanish
on a secondary road
in Auvergne
it whines
it's never regular
I seem to be lost
but I like
irregular cycles
I'd almost give you
a solar clock
but you're blowing
on my neck too much
I can't hear
you seem to have
left the sun
behind in a closet
you say that it's far
yet I would gladly give you
a sun
it seems that it travels
in my suitcase
it reaches
the Alps
and even Scandinavia
before me

I can't really
turn around
there's nothing discreet
about the wind effect
I'm just saying
but you're not making
any effort
it coughs above my ear
it scratches my edges
it sneezes everywhere
it coughs
it hiccups
the cycle is irregular
I'm rooted in a place
where moving forward
isn't calculated
I don't calculate time
my clock is solar
it's obvious
I don't have an allergy
but because the angel
is allergic
I prefer to steer clear
of pistachios
have I told you
how green
grates on me?

Have I told you
how green
upsets me?
Well, I've changed my mind
let them keep their green
I'll decide for myself
I like green
perhaps the angel
will like pistachios
it seems one outgrows
allergies
I'm not allergic
to the cold
it's just that you're coughing
inside me
that I forget everything
that forgetting everything
keeps me from thinking
keeps me from hearing
keeps me
from hearing the story
of your mother
the tea she would prefer
I can't turn around
something
keeps me from turning around
stay where you are

don't go further than above the ear

don't cough on my face

wait until it's less

humid

I'll hear you better

when the wind effect

has gotten the better of my neck

all things pass

you'll see

all things pass

the cycle is irregular

I count correctly

even when it's cold

everything changes

I tell you some things

to reassure you

there are many things

in my suitcase

the sun

is a metaphor

vitamin D

isn't a metaphor

everything that can be calculated

forgets the metaphor

I don't calculate the cycle

my breath

is irregular

when I move forward
I make no decisions
it's the cough on my neck
that moves forward
I don't hear you
the partition is obvious
I don't hear you
perhaps you're no longer
saying anything
I no longer hear anything
around me
it doesn't whine
I no longer see dancing
the clocks no longer lead
the dial has taken time off
perhaps you're no longer
saying anything
it doesn't sneeze
it no longer hums
I didn't count
the last stanza
my trunk might
turn around

I met you
in disorder.

You met me
in disorder

did I even
shake your hand?

Your hair
was a mess

you were so talkative

so talkative.

If only you knew
how your lack of order
amuses me

what a strange idea
to tune up
in order to exchange
hellos

you were emerging from a long tunnel

or you were at the end

I'd forgotten what time we were meeting

the potatoes were sweet

the quay perfectly erased

I don't remember

hearing cars

go by

nor passersby

you were waiting for me at the end of the tunnel

but what wasn't planned

were the sweet potatoes

and the silence

the silence

that isn't trying to fill itself

the silence in disorder

that makes me forget to shake your hand

because for me

it was certainly not

the first

time.

I saw you arrive in the distance
your echo
extended
from arid mountain
to sea

certain things
are not to be questioned
they resound
like an announcement

not having seen you

arrive in the distance

something

in the thick

dust

of the horizon

preceded

me

from your echo

you don't even tremble

you don't even tremble

your ample stride
my staccato pattern

trees pass me by
boats pass you by

it's not certain we see
the same thing
we don't hear
the same thing

so speak to me

about the braised endives

they like

where you're from

here it's the onions

the onions

that bring us together

the hanging peppers and the onions

what happens
happens first
on the tongue

the tongue's
memory
precedes us

the red onions
preceding
the tongue

there's nothing disordered
in what comes
how it comes
it comes just right

it exhales right
it alternates right
it pants right
it dances right
it is announced.

2|1

I'm rooted in movement

I'm rooted in movement

I'm rooted in movement

I'm rooted in movement
this phenomenon is improbable

It's improbable
I'm rooted in resonance

I'm rooted in transparency
branches glide over me

I'm rooted in resonance
I scrutinize all that's being whispered
on my neck

I'm rooted in transparency
I exert the highest tension
I tremble

I'm rooted in movement
have I ever known
how to be rooted in movement?

I'm rooted in transparency
what's revealed of me
is revealed of us

                                        I've been rooted in movement
                                        for so long
                                        that I'm rooted in movement

I'm rooted in resonance
what passes through me
mirrors what's coming

I'm rooted in movement
when the round opens
I'm rooted in movement
when the triangle opens
I'm rooted in movement
when the line closes
I'm rooted in movement
when your eyes release me
I'm rooted in movement
when you make me wait
I'm rooted in movement
when it topples
I'm rooted in movement
when you catch a cold
I'm rooted in movement
when your fingers brush against me
I'm rooted in movement
when your voice falls silent
I'm rooted in movement
when your curve bends
I'm rooted in movement.

My lips even
have seen you arrive in the distance

the crackling of leaves
behind my neck

the horizon
stretches

the bridges come in succession
they straddle me
the arches straddle me

you split the span
the span of the arch
the span of the bridge
you straddle me
in the distance

arches all around me

even my lips
have seen you arrive in the distance

the breach becomes a sphere

when it topples

when it approaches

when it shoves

the sphere expands

even my lips

even my lips

in the distance

something quivers
that you don't see
and is

even my lips
in the distance
even my lips
see you arrive

you arrive

around

the sphere

expands

time

expands

the oily surface

expands

even my lips

my lips

in the distance

the trunks blush
in the distance

you go past the boats
I go past the trees
the sails unfurl
even my lips
even my lips
around
it won't be too late
you arrive
in the distance
it won't be too late

I see you
the dream
the attraction
awakens
the faraway nights

when on the oily surface
the faraway night
expands

you don't tremble
I no longer tremble

something quivers
that is

you're not late
my lips even
in the distance
quiver
from time
from time
that expands
still

a river

quivers

under the blushing

trunks

a river

retraces

its flow

even

in the distance

even

in the distance

the river

swelling

in the distance

you arrive

the flows

merge

you arrive

a river

arrives

a river

arrives

a river

arrives

a river

arrives

a river

arrives

a river

arrives

a river

arrives

a river

arrives

a river

arrives

a river

arrives

a river

arrives

and then the streets

and then the parks

and then your room

and then your head

I'm not afraid of emptiness

the breach is a distant moment

a sun that's reborn

in the fresh surface

of a silent winter morning

where I want to think about the nothingness that opens

where I want to think about the space that remains

anything's possible

it fades

gently

it expands

it fades

gently

and then the streets
and then the parks
and then your room
and then your head.

It's above all
confusion
that knocks you over
and drops you
in the right place
on the right edge
the end of the quay
that breaks away
and opens you

it's confusion

that makes us two

it's between two

that time

is born

edgeless time

fleeting time

that creates the breach

the lasting breach

there where space

can finally be

touched

between

and between

that touches

there

where

to join.

Something quivers
between
that I don't see
but that I know.

There's a lucid moment
when the journey doesn't wait

I'm not afraid of the emptiness
the quivering
of the wave
inhabits.

It's a moment in movement
in which to dive.

I dove
I've been gifted
to see
to hear
I've been gifted
to love.

I move forward
in the river moving forward
I'm rooted in movement
time passes through me
beings pass through me
they are me
I am them

I'm rooted in movement
when I dive
I resurface
when I arrive
I'm already far

I'm rooted in movement
my steps don't land
they dance
in the elsewhere

I'm rooted in movement
but when I'm rooted
in movement
I unroll
the horizon.

I've been gifted
to live
what
in the white dawn
awakens.

TRACES

1

I don't sleep at night when light falls.

When darkness falls, dust rises over me, tenacious dust invading my nostrils and settling, thick, on everything serving as companions.

I don't sleep at night. When silence falls, faces resurface in my memory, also those I've never seen.

Faces are rooted inside me, all that passed by me during the day and others I haven't seen pass by.

I don't sleep at night, my ears are so sensitive, they hear all the din of the day and, at night, they regurgitate the sounds, they analyze them.

Each sound must resume its place, in silence. I arrange them by thickness and color, also by effects . . . it's not very scientific, it's my way of passing the time because I don't sleep. That's the story I tell, it seems more logical.

For, in fact, it's all of this that keeps me awake, the jumbled sounds I must organize when night falls, the jumbled faces deserving of a little more attention.

It's so sad—or so something, I can't think of the word, there's no exact word—to not greet a passing face with dignity, be it a crazed crowd, even crowds need to be honored, face after face, one after the other, especially crowds, that's why I don't blame the dust for burning my nostrils, it reminds me not to sleep, that my attention is incomplete, that all crowds deserve full attention.

2

All around you there's a cloud of scarlet shadows vanishing in the setting sun, a cloud of shifting shadows, a cloud.

All around you there are vertical shadows, tilted shadows that sometimes distend, that thicken and invade, shadows that lean against angles you're unaware of, splits, skirmishes.

Shadows jostling you in unison. Sometimes humid, seldom synchronous, mostly vertical, veeeeerticaaaaal . . .

That's what holds you back.

There are trunks all around you, perfectly uniform, a forest of trunks from a faraway time that some consider sacred.
It depends on what, it depends on whom, it depends on what that entails, on many other things.
Here there are sacred souls behind the trunks, the sacred trunks of the sacred trees, in the sacred forest you're passing through.

It depends on how you pass through.

All around you there are walls, walls that have lost their verticality, lost their suppleness, walls that no one wants to climb . . . who would want to climb an inert mountain?

Coarse walls whose gray verges on apoplectic, walls piled near the trunks, near the shadows, near the trees, near the inert clouds,
against the open angles of the forest passing through you.

It depends on how you pass through.

3

Trunks sink into the water, I can't make out the roots, I can't tell for sure if they're floating. Something floats around, frail legs take root and drift in unison with the water's movement.

All life is movement, it's one of those obvious facts we nevertheless should remember each day, be told each day, and notice each moment.

The landscape is peaceful, it's only conjecture. There are no waves, the tide is low, no child wanders around in the swamp, the sky is low, the sails seem motionless.

Withdrawn in this way, the sea reveals nothing of roots, and yet everything moves, everything is a tangle of pulses, memories, presences, lives, questions.

The sea withdraws, I don't move forward, a door approaches my immobility, furrows emerge from this visible silence. I don't see what lies in the swamp, I don't move. I listen to silence with my eyes.

Trunks like keepers of oblivion
remind me of what is missing
remind me of missed meetings
those to come I'll choose to miss
those to come I'll brush against
and all those I will not understand.

On each emerging crest
in each optical illusion
roads rise again
white routes intertwining
clay routes awakening the ground
sandy routes upending the desert.

On each mirage,
each movement of a moored boat,
the furrow awakens.

4

Sea routes dissolve in the waves
your pulse knows them by heart
sea routes leave imprints in salt
your muscles know them by heart
every unknown footstep of every one of your ancestors
is engraved even deeper into your body.

The tide will return, the tide will float the footprints
again, myriad footprints on the motionless surface.

Footprints on footprints on threads on lines on voices
on the water's surface.

The motionless footprint breathes within
your motionless eyes breathe within
your motionless body opens the sails
within.

I'm not trying to climb a wall /// especially not if it's inert /// I'm not trying to climb the sea /// I don't want to remember that the sea is a wall /// I'm not trying to cross the sea /// I don't want to remember that the sea doesn't want me to cross it /// I watch the world move in my thorax /// boats by the dozens make semicircles /// break the lines /// intersect routes /// zigzag on the surface that seems motionless.

And, without noticing, kiss the sand, enter the shore's body by a clear-cut hollow, a sound, a word with no possible translation, an escaped language, a language that flows through the fingers.

I want to enter the earth through the water
and the water through the water's footprint.

5

The town is a tongue the sea takes by storm
the town is an overburdened tongue at the story's border.
At the border of the border
the town overflows
its tongue is swollen.

You position yourself at its tip, at the place where restless
verbs turn up.

the tip against the sea swells up
the sea against the tip chills your pulse
the pulse of the swelling tongue
the sea against the tip of your tongue calls out
the tongue against the sea unburdens itself.

My body sways
on the midday axis
it loses the North
it sways.

Vertigo lies in wait
dust lies in wait
car horns lie in wait
wheels, wheels
wheels in all sizes
lie in wait for me
and the gutters!

The gutter lies in wait for me!

My body sways, evades, head wedged under the barely
unbearable weight, I bend just enough to avoid erasure,
no erasure on my curve, I don't waddle, I cut a fine
figure, I sway just enough to avoid the wheel, the small
wheel, the large wheel and the gutter that lies in wait
for me, that still lies in wait for me,
it's my preference.

On the midday axis, vertigo skims past
I will not reach the tip
I will not unburden myself any time soon.

My hands sway
neither left nor right
their movement is more complex
did you think that I came from an assembly line?

Oh! If you stayed there staring at me . . .
If you had that patience, in the burning midday axis, you
would see how far my hands sway into your pupils.

6

A finger realigns the threads /// a finger cuts /// a finger inverts /// a finger presses /// a finger slips /// a finger goes and comes back /// a finger inverts the threads /// a finger flits /// a finger gives you a drink /// a finger pulls fabric over the baby's cheek /// a finger smiles /// a finger tastes /// a finger measures /// a finger dips into mercury /// a finger spools threads /// a finger follows you /// a finger measures you and in measuring you, it measures the distance /// a finger scrutinizes you /// a finger asks you the question again /// a finger spins the threads /// a finger shakes /// a finger planes /// a finger wipes the corner of the eye /// a finger extends the invitation /// a finger passes through you.

My hands sway, they endlessly repeat the same gestures, they're inscribed in me.

Gesture is multifold.

Within gestures, there's a pileup of gestures, which I repeat. I don't remember learning them, they entered me, by magic or necessity.

There was no forced entry between us, no rape.

The gestures I repeat are like silence, they don't bother me, they have their own life, I have mine which observes the swamp, the dawdling child in the swamp collecting what he shouldn't collect on this surface loaded with what shouldn't be there.

The wandering child collects.

Gesture is multifold
it's silent inside me
and that's how I see
That's how I see you
multifold.
That's how I touch you.

The motionless surface
vibrating, vibrating
making a sail within
breathes within.

7

Rowboats sway against the tongue.

Under the rowboats, there are footsteps.
There are trunks rooted under the tongue, there are trees floating on the tongue, walls for diving into memory. There are movable bridges and white routes, water routes overloaded with footsteps, motionless gestures, motionless thoughts, painless thwacks.

There are motionless civilizations planted there, on the crest of a dormant coliseum.

Arches sway in the passing shimmer
gestures repeat themselves
fingers repeat the refrain
the midday axis dozes off
sleep dives between two lines.

All around you shadows sway when you see through
the trees, the trees of sacred wood.
In this optical illusion, there is that endless moment.

8

It's a cloud of pilgrims moving toward us, the whiteness of their robes scarcely matters, the scattered threads scarcely matter. Their skins don't show the same marks, nor the same lines.
A cloud of pilgrims is moving toward us, no one knows in what direction, no one knows for what homage.

You saw them coming toward you, their footsteps calm and slow, like people who have come a long way know how to walk, from a distance defying the imagination, from a distance outside any aerial reference point.

The pilgrims walk, and like the ones arrived in Papua, in Siberia, or in the Brazilian jungle, they walk, they know the paths by heart.

No elevation stands up to the pilgrims, no turbulent river, no blast of sea air.

In turbulence the pilgrims move forward, with slow and silent gestures, they glide in the blurred vision of the mist they stir up.

You see them move forward, the pilgrims have neither height, nor age, nor gender, nor color. And yet, you see they're everything at once, you see they're a merging multitude now adopting the same facial expression, the same muscular contraction.

It's as if they were plugged into a different frequency, when they move forward like this, with the same stride. The incoming flow of fabric you imagine as white moves forward.

You know they're not white, but the wave crashing down on you like a steady and uniform blast of air lets you see these taut bodies draped in white and momentum.

9

You don't want the momentum to worry you, you let the momentum come to you and you think that every momentum is life and death, that every momentum is at first life, is at first a wager you make on life, a wager you win on yourself.
You don't want the momentum to immobilize you, you know that all breath of life is engraved on the cliff.
All breath of life is engraved on the rough and damaged tip of every story.

The wave descends upon you,
you walk in the other direction.

The wave parts as it reaches you, so you become a knot,
a trunk, a menhir, a well.
The wave is getting around you, it's all around you,
you are on the inside.

You walk in the other direction but a part of yourself is
already walking with the pilgrims, you have no choice
but to give in to the wave still getting around you, still
taking care to protect the trunk, the menhir, the well, the
unfathomable knot.

You let a part of yourself go along with the wave,
you move in the other direction.

The halo of the wave hypnotizes you,
you have no choice but to slow down.

The halo of the wave hypnotizes you, and this silent cloud seems to carry so many stories, so many words, so many faces, so many landscapes, so many languages, so very many.

This cloud speaks in its silent and steadfast progression, silence speaks.

10

Seconds or minutes go by.

You can't tell how long it takes for the wave to calmly break on you, the halo to move forward, the other part of yourself to depart in the other direction.

The wave passes through you, it seems to pass through you even as it fades into the horizon and you move forward, alone, in the other direction.

You don't know how long it takes to pass through your body nor what dwells within you when you move forward, alone, in the other direction.

Now that you're walking alone again, you become the wave, you become the deep breath of the wave.

You think of all the trunks
all the menhirs
all the wells
all the unfathomable knots
you must get around
with care.

You hear all the axes around you, all the lines of the great web joining, one by one, the gathered cloud.

You think you are your own pilgrim cloud climbing back up the other axis on the opposite side, that you are also the wave falling back in the other direction.

You are the direction and the other directions
no geography is contradictory
no wave is more worthy than another wave.

The waves tangle up and intersect, the way rowboats meet, and also those footsteps we think are lost on surfaces that sand and water and also other things will inevitably cover.

Everything in us ends up being covered
everything in us remains.

Everything remains if we know how to carefully get around
trees
menhirs
voices
faces
and the stories of other beings
and also other things.

11

In the space between us, there's so much.
There's what's said and never will be said.
There's what's written and never will be written.
There's what's thought, there's also what's neglected.

In the space between us, there's a cloud of impossibles
like birdsong we can't transcribe.

There's the weight of time, there's the weight of histories
we don't share.

In the space between us, there are also the accidents overwhelming us, those that sometimes open a door. We sometimes see this door and sometimes choose to take it.

If I speak to you, I speak through what we lack. This lack is our chance, the only true excuse for venturing out on the road.
The impulse comes from what we call instinct, virus, inner voice.
But isn't what we lack what we most want to make exist?

We draw lines where they weigh us down.

And because we drew them, now we can
erase them, letting the sea return to its peaceful swaying.

I came from an earlier time
to remind you of the promise of dawn.
Every child
is the child of the renewed dawn
who will teach us again the profound Song
the intimate rhythm of our cells.

I came from that time that amasses horizons
and sifts through them
one by one, with care
giving each its measure.

I came from the Algiers door
to reach the peak of Toubkal.
I came from the manuscripts of Timbuktu
To bring the word to the sages of Kilimanjaro.
I came from the N'Djamena door
I almost got sunstroke in Cotonou.
I was madly in love in Zanzibar.
I came through the Cape Town door
unable to read the meaning of stars
I dreamt of crossing that triangle
that could take me from Cairo
to Saguia el Hamra.

I entered one hundred times through the Gorée door
where I left a rosary of tears.

I entered through Gorée where I tried to come back to life.

Solio . . .
I entered through so many doors
passed through so much of myself.

Solio . . .
Everywhere I was told about wounds
and pardons
those we no longer wait for
those that one day will come
those we'll pretend not to owe.

People often spoke to me straight in the eyes.

Solio
I came back from my crossing
to tell you my last prayer
Solio
God is a black woman with legs covered in soot
Solio
make sure to honor these black legs covered in soot
Solio
and so, you will be.

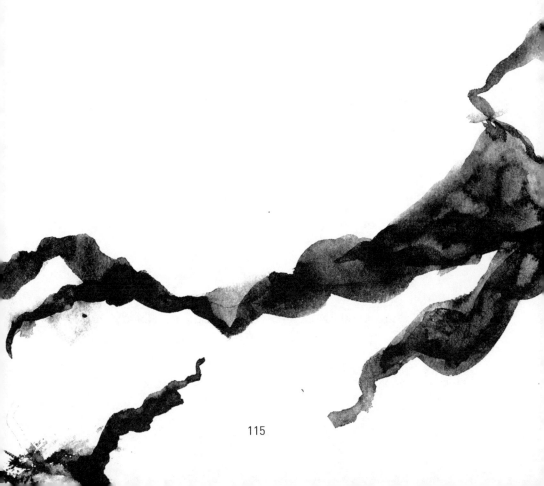

THE ENCOUNTER AS LEVER

A NOTE ON *QUAY 2/1*

Creating—writing—is a solitary endeavor that can't do without the world of the Other. It's born of seeing, listening, tension. It's born of an interaction you might imagine as chemical because the logic of the visible is unable to explain it.

The encounter is often silent, with the work of art, with the being, their voice, their presence.

Silently we pass by the one who nourishes us, we do not alter this dialog of a shared offering.

Creating in a group of two or three is nothing short of a miracle, a high-risk exercise that you really only venture into with someone in whom trust runs deep, or you share a common way of looking at things.

When I met violinist Marianne Piketty in February 2017, it was initially about creating a performance to be viewed by a small audience of a hundred people, but something extremely rare opened up between us: the act of listening, fully engaged listening.

And it became obvious that we had to take this listening much further.

And through what other chemistry! When Marianne had the intuition to invite theorbist Bruno Helstroffer to join the adventure, another axis opened up within myself, between us. I confess to not knowing what falls under the "Us."

Together we made our way.

From Lyon to Algiers, across unchartered territories. We knew that the three of us wanted to build something together, that a rare spark had been ignited, but we didn't force anything upon ourselves. Neither theme nor framework nor roles. We opened a common page and allowed ourselves to explore off the beaten path. We had only one "constraint": participate in an artist residency, followed by a performance at the School of Music and Dance in Trappes-en-Yvelines in March 2018.

The least I can say is that we pushed limits. Both internally and externally. It wasn't about creating an umpteenth musical reading, but to allow ourselves to be shaped by what was growing among us.

Stratum after stratum, the framework was built and that's how *Quay 2|1* was conceived—the performance as well as the book you're holding in your hands.

I felt it was important that the work feed off the music's soul, but also be a poem, free of any context.

I listened to what was rustling and that we shared. Marianne and Bruno are an essential part of what I have written. Together we abolished boundaries.

They were a powerful lever and I had to hold nothing back.

Samira Negrouche
Algiers, January 27, 2019

A NOTE ON *TRACES*

This text was written during the course of 2019 as a co-creation with choreographer Fatou Cissé. Our collaboration was initiated and facilitated through the Univers des mots festival, and was supported by a residency program at La Chartreuse in Villeneuve-lès-Avignon (through the Odyssée program). After a five-week residency in Conakry, two public performances took place in November 2019 as part of the Univers des mots festival. Thanks to everyone who made this project possible.

Samira Negrouche

TRANSLATOR'S ACKNOWLEDGMENTS

I am deeply grateful to Catherine Maigret Kellogg for being the best sounding board a translator could ever wish for, as we navigated some of the more challenging texts in these pages. Thanks, too, to Gerald Maa for his helpful input about retaining the strangeness of the original's syntax, as well as to my husband, Ted Miller, for patiently listening and providing input into my word-choice dilemmas during our daily dog walks. Special thanks are also due to the poet herself, Samira Negrouche, for her generosity and patience as we worked together to find the mot juste. I am forever grateful to the brilliant team at Seagull Books, including Naveen Kishore, for believing in me and my work, and Sunandini Banerjee, for her magnificent cover design, as well as the artwork that graces these pages. In addition, I am indebted to the editors of *Modern Poetry in Translation* and the *Hopkins Review* for granting permission to draw on much shorter versions of the translator's foreword, as well as to the editors of the following literary journals in which excerpts from these translations first appeared, some in earlier versions:

The Arkansas International	*Hunger Mountain*
AzonaL	*The Michigan Quarterly Review*
Five Points	*Modern Poetry in Translation*
The Georgia Review	*The Offing*
The High Window	*A Public Space*
The Hopkins Review	*West Branch*

The quote from Margaret Sayers Peden originally appeared in an interview with James Hoggard in *Translation Review*, issue 56(1) (1998).